IAN EDELMAN

Discovering Avebury

SHIRE PUBLICATIONS LTD

Contents

Introduction 3
1. The Avebury Monument 5
2. The village of Avebury 11
3. The parish church of St James 14
4. Avebury Manor 17
5. Alexander Keiller Museum 18
6. Avebury Dovecote 18
7. The Great Barn Museum of Wiltshire Folk Life 20
Further reading 24
Useful information 24

 First published 1985; reprinted 1985, 1987, 1988, 1989 and 1992. Number 280 in the Discovering series. ISBN 0 85263 766 7.

Printed in Great Britain by C. I. Thomas & Sons (Haverfordwest) Ltd, Press Buildings, Merlins Bridge, Haverfordwest, Dyfed SA61 1XF.

The bank and ditch of the north-east quadrant.

Introduction

Avebury lies in the Kennet valley approximately 7 miles (11 km) west of Marlborough and 9 miles (14 km) north-east of Devizes on the chalklands of the Marlborough Downs. This part of north Wiltshire is characterised by an undulating landscape, punctuated with small clusters of beech trees which stand majestically on the tops of the windswept downs. This rolling downland is particularly rich in monuments of the prehistoric period. Of all these archaeological sites, the finest is to be found at Avebury. The small village of Avebury stands at the centre of one of the most impressive of all the ancient monuments in Great Britain. It is a late neolithic religious site of international importance, forming the centre of a unique complex of prehistoric monuments.

The main A4361 not only runs through the village but also cuts a zigzag path through the centre of the prehistoric monument on its way between Swindon and Devizes. The A4, the old coaching route between London and Bristol, passes to the south to within 1 mile (1.6 km) of Avebury. This once far busier road is linked to the A4361 by the West Kennet Avenue. The visitor approaching Avebury from this direction is drawn onward by the parallel pairs of sarsen stones which line the field on the west side of the road. From the east and from the west Avebury can be approached only on foot. A footpath leads from the adjacent village of Avebury Trusloe and crosses the river Kennet before joining the High Street. A short length of road, which soon becomes a farm track, runs east out of the village to join the ancient Ridgeway track about 1½ miles (2.4 km) away.

There cannot be many visitors who remain unmoved by their first sight of these ancient and mysterious circles of enormous stones and the massive surrounding earthwork. Many of the great stone monoliths have been pulled down and destroyed, so that one can only wonder at the former magnificence of the monument. John Aubrey, the seventeenth-century antiquary, compared Avebury as a cathedral to the parish church of Stonehenge. Although Avebury is still considered by many people to be far more magnificent and awe-inspiring, it has never received as much attention as Stonehenge. This has allowed Avebury to remain relatively unspoilt. Long after the rites and rituals associated with the Avebury circle had been forgotten, settlement became established in and around the monument. Unlike Stonehenge, which stands alone and in isolation on Salisbury Plain, the Avebury circle is now an integral part of a living rural community. Houses, an inn and village shops are to be found within the perimeter of the prehistoric monument. There are also two museums, a manor house and a fine church.

(Above) The Diamond Stone is reputed to turn full circle on its axis at midnight.

(Below) The Devil's Chair, one of the stones flanking the south entrance.

1. The Avebury Monument

The Avebury Monument is a henge consisting of an outer bank and an inner ditch. Within this enormous circular enclosure is an outer circle of stones and inside this are two smaller circles of stones. Excavation has shown that the two inner circles are perhaps older by several hundred years than the main circle, the bank and the ditch.

The earthwork forms a slightly irregular circle enclosing an area of about 28½ acres (11.5 ha). Its diameter is just over 500 yards (450 m) and the circumference along the top of the bank is about 1550 yards (1450 m). The bank was once taller and the ditch deeper. However, during the intervening thousands of years, erosion has weathered the bank and silted the ditch. The bank was constructed from the chalk dug to make the ditch. Antler picks and ox shoulder blades were the tools used for this immense feat of earth moving. Four entrance gaps were left in the earthwork, roughly corresponding to the cardinal points of the compass.

About one hundred huge sarsen boulders, weighing up to 60 tons each, were used for the outer circle of stones. Unlike the sarsens of Stonehenge, none of the Avebury stones has been 'dressed' or shaped, but they do appear to have been selected for their shape. They fall into two basic types, tall and straight-sided or diamond-shaped. Sarsen is a particularly hard sandstone which can still be found occurring naturally as huge slabs on the ground surface of the Marlborough Downs near Avebury. It is possible that wooden sledges pulled by men or perhaps oxen were used to drag the sarsen blocks over a mile across sometimes awkward terrain. Once at Avebury, the stone was levered off its sledge. Leather ropes, levers and timber bracing were then used to raise each stone into an upright position in its pre-dug hole in the chalk. Smaller pieces of stone were finally packed into the hole around the base to make it secure.

The largest stones were placed in pairs flanking the four entrances. The two stones at the south entrance can still be seen to one side of the main road. One of these stones is known as the Devil's Chair. It is said that if a person sits on the small ledge or seat on the southern face of the stone, smoke can be seen coming from the small hole above! The Diamond Stone (also known as the Swindon Stone), which is the only remaining stone of the pair at the northern entrance, is reputed either to cross the road at midnight to search for its missing partner, or to turn a full 360 degrees on its base at the same witching hour.

Within the interior of the circle were two smaller circles, originally of about thirty stones each. At the centre of the northern circle was an arrangement of three large stones forming three sides of a square. William Stukeley, the eighteenth-century antiquary, named these the Cove, although the third stone had already been removed in his time.

The southern circle also has stones within its interior. A straight line of sarsen stones with additional stones at either end stands in the western part of the circle. At the centre stood a tall stone which Stukeley called the Obelisk. It has now gone, but its location is shown by a large concrete marker. The village maypole used to be erected nearby. The Ring Stone is a broken stump which stands to the south of the southern circle and is all that remains of a once larger stone which had a natural hole through it.

The West Kennet Avenue is a pair of parallel lines of large sarsen stones which originally ran from the southern entrance of the circle for about 1½ miles (2.4 km) to the Sanctuary on Overton Hill. This small site consists of concentric rings of stones and post holes now indicated by concrete markers. The post holes of the Sanctuary are not all of one period of prehistory but represent several phases of building. Stukeley also recorded evidence of a stone avenue which led from the western entrance of the Avebury circle past Beckhampton. Two large sarsens, known as Adam and Eve, which stand isolated in a field near Beckhampton, may have been part of this lost avenue.

The Avebury Monument was probably completed by about 2400 BC. We can never know the exact purpose of its construction, but it must have been an important place of worship. The nature of the religious ceremonies associated with the circle is unknown. The builders of the circle must have been inspired with a zealous enthusiasm which fired them to execute such a monumental task. It could not have been undertaken without a well organised political and economic system capable of harnessing the considerable manpower resources needed to construct the earthwork and erect the stones. The size and scale of the monument remain as a testimony of the labour and skills of ancient man.

Following its abandonment about one thousand years after its construction, the Avebury circle probably remained unused and relatively undamaged. The monument has impressed the inquisitive for many centuries. Visitors to Avebury during the Roman period of the mid first to late fourth centuries AD are evidenced by the quantities of broken pottery sherds found in the silt layers of the ditch. It is likely that they would have seen the circle, perhaps somewhat overgrown, but largely unchanged.

There is some archaeological evidence to suggest Saxon occupation or settlement in Avebury as early as the sixth century AD. The parish church of St James has late Saxon architectural features dating to the tenth century. A written reference in an

(Above) The view towards the southern circle with the south entrance beyond.

(Below) The West Kennet Avenue.

assize roll of 1289 refers to Avebury as 'Waleditch'. This probably derives from the Saxon words meaning 'dyke of the Britons'. This Saxon name appears to have been used concurrently with the present name, occurring as 'Avreberie' in Domesday of 1086. 'Afa's burg or fortification' is suggested as a possible translation.

In 1114 some of the royal lands held in Avebury were given to the Benedictine monastery of St George de Boscherville in Normandy. A small priory was built on or close by the site of the present manor house. During the twelfth century the small church was enlarged and the interior of the circle put to the plough. By this time the village of Avebury was well established. Fear of the dark forces of paganism, for which it was believed the circle had been built, had until the middle ages allowed the stones to remain unmolested. This is exemplified by the huge stone at the south entrance which is still called the Devil's Chair. At this time we find evidence of a systematic programme to destroy the devil's work.

Many stones were pushed over into pits and buried. One of the fallen stones in the south-west quadrant is now called the Barber Stone. It gained this name because of the grisly find made during its excavation in 1938. The skeleton of an itinerant barber-surgeon was found crushed beneath the stone. His body could not be removed and was left to be buried with the stone. His iron scissors and probe were found beside him and a pouch containing coins dating to about 1320 provides evidence of the date of his death, and thus also the date of the toppling of the stone. By the middle of the fourteenth century the destruction ceased and the remaining stones were left.

Avebury was first brought to public attention by John Leland in about 1541. William Camden made brief reference in *Britannia* published in 1610. The first full account does not occur until the middle of the seventeenth century, when John Aubrey visited the site and made sketches and plans. His study of Avebury produced sufficient interest for Charles II to visit the monument to see it for himself.

During the latter half of the seventeenth century the destruction of the circle commenced yet again, as much to provide building materials and to clear the land for ploughing as for religious reasons.

The stones were toppled into pits filled with burning straw. The application of cold water followed by a battering with sledgehammers created structural weaknesses which shattered the stones into manageable blocks. Many blocks of stone in the houses of Avebury are said to show a reddening from fire. It was during this period that buildings were first erected in the interior of the circle. A large sarsen standing at the western entrance has

(Above) The south-west quadrant.

(Below) Silbury Hill.

now been partly reconstructed from broken fragments. These were found during demolition of a cottage, which had been built around the remaining stone and incorporated several of the smaller lumps in its walls.

Between 1719 and 1724 William Stukeley made detailed records, drawings and plans of the circle, which were published in 1743 as *Abury, a Temple of the British Druids.* Stukeley witnessed the destruction during his visits to Avebury. His records have proved to be of immense importance in providing information that would otherwise have been lost following the destruction of the circle. The North Circle, and much of the South Circle and Outer Ring had already been destroyed. The tearing down of the stones gradually became less frequent and had completely ceased by the early nineteenth century.

By the twentieth century the circle had become obscured beneath many cottages, hedges and trees. Between 1934 and 1939 about half the circle and the West Kennet Avenue were excavated by Alexander Keiller. He erected fallen stones, replaced missing stones with concrete markers, demolished a number of buildings and removed many of the trees and bushes which had overgrown parts of the circle. Keiller was heir to a flourishing marmalade business; with his financial resources he was able to purchase the entire monument.

In 1942 the circle passed into the ownership and protection of the National Trust and is now under the guardianship of English Heritage, which is also responsible for Windmill Hill, West Kennet Long Barrow and Silbury Hill. These ancient monuments are all to be found a little more than a mile from Avebury and are all open to the public. **Windmill Hill** is a neolithic 'causewayed enclosure' located to the north-west of Avebury. The **West Kennet Long Barrow** is just south of the A4 between Beckhampton and West Kennet. It is a neolithic burial mound about 330 feet (100 m) long. The five burial chambers contained the bones of at least forty-six people. Close by, on the north side of the A4, is **Silbury Hill.** This enormous man-made neolithic hill remains an enigma, as archaeological excavation has failed to uncover its purpose. There are a number of well written books containing more detailed information on these monuments and the Avebury circle. Most of these publications are available in Avebury.

2. The village of Avebury

Far fewer houses now remain within the perimeter of the circle than at the beginning of the twentieth century. Alexander Keiller embarked upon a scheme to remove all standing buildings from the circle in order to afford the visitor an uninterrupted view of the monument. A row of four cottages once lined the east side of the Swindon Road in the north-east quadrant, and two thatched cottages were demolished on the corner opposite the Red Lion. A pair of turnpike cottages were removed from the end of the West Kennet Avenue. This policy of destruction was continued until recent times by the National Trust. All buildings within and beyond the circle are now protected as part of the Avebury Conservation Area.

Almost at the centre of the circle on the crossroads stands the **Red Lion Inn.** This old thatched building has been much altered and added to over the years. In one corner of the car park are the remains of an old cider press and a millstone. Neither of these was used in the village, but they were put there during the 1950s as decoration for the car park. A ghostly coach and horses are said to have been heard to clatter on to the cobblestones outside the Red Lion. An old well can be seen inside the building.

Avebury has frequently attracted the producers of archaeological documentary films. The Red Lion was, however, used as the location for filming the 1933 Ben Travers farce *A Cuckoo in the Nest,* and in the early 1970s the television ghost drama *Children of the Stones* was filmed in the village.

Over the road from the Red Lion is Green Street. The last thatched building on the right-hand side was the **carpenter's cottage.** The wooden building to the front housed the sawpit, where lengths of timber were once laboriously cut.

Towards the centre of the circle, on the same side of the road, is the **Congregational chapel.** A meeting house was first established in Avebury in 1670. However, this building, with its tiny graveyard in front, dates from the eighteenth century. During the nineteenth century the chapel was enlarged and the roof raised. The schoolroom at the rear was also added. As well as this chapel and the parish church, Avebury also had a Baptist chapel, which stood on the site of the present small central car park.

Crossing the main road, the visitor can pause on the small triangular grassed traffic island at the top of the High Street. This is the village green and must be one of the smallest there is.

The public lavatories stand next door to the Red Lion. These were once the coach house and stables for the **The Lodge,** which is the large rendered and painted house on the left, built in the eighteenth century. In front of these buildings, from the Red

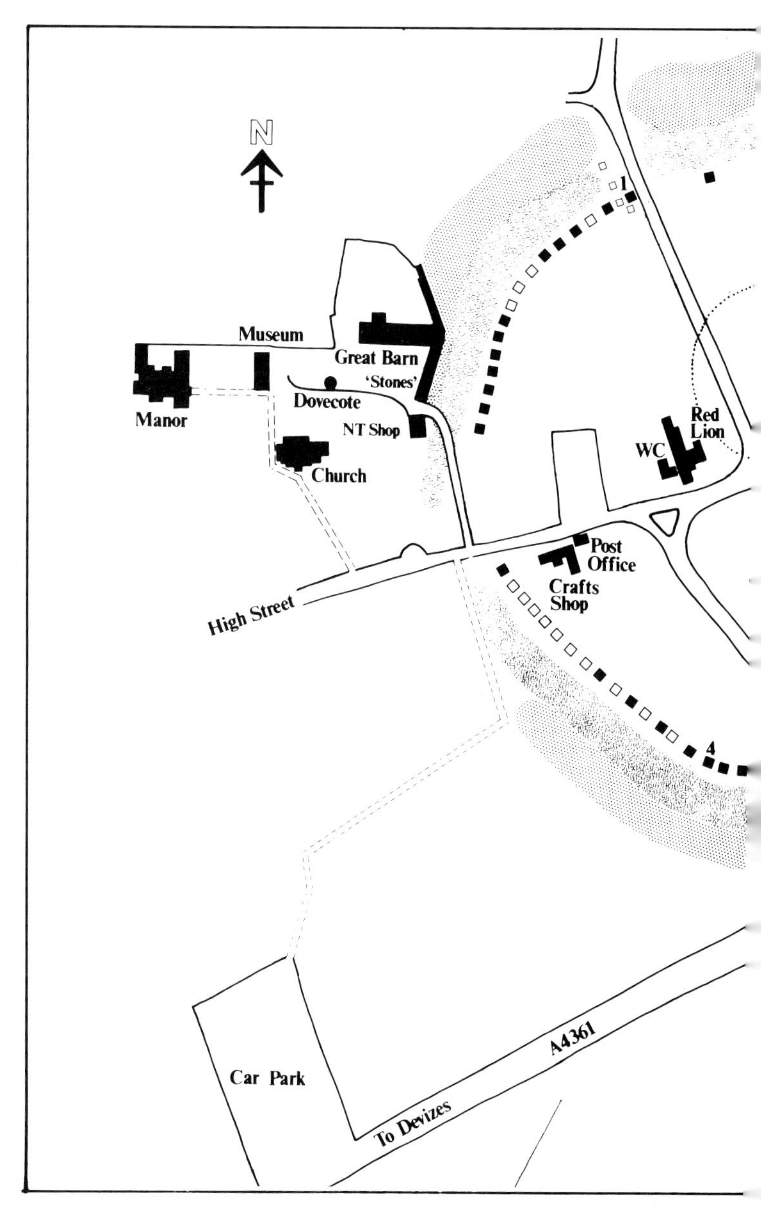
N
1
Museum
Great Barn
'Stones'
Dovecote
NT Shop
Manor
Church
Red
Lion
WC
Post
Office
Crafts
Shop
High Street
4
Car Park
A4361
To Devizes

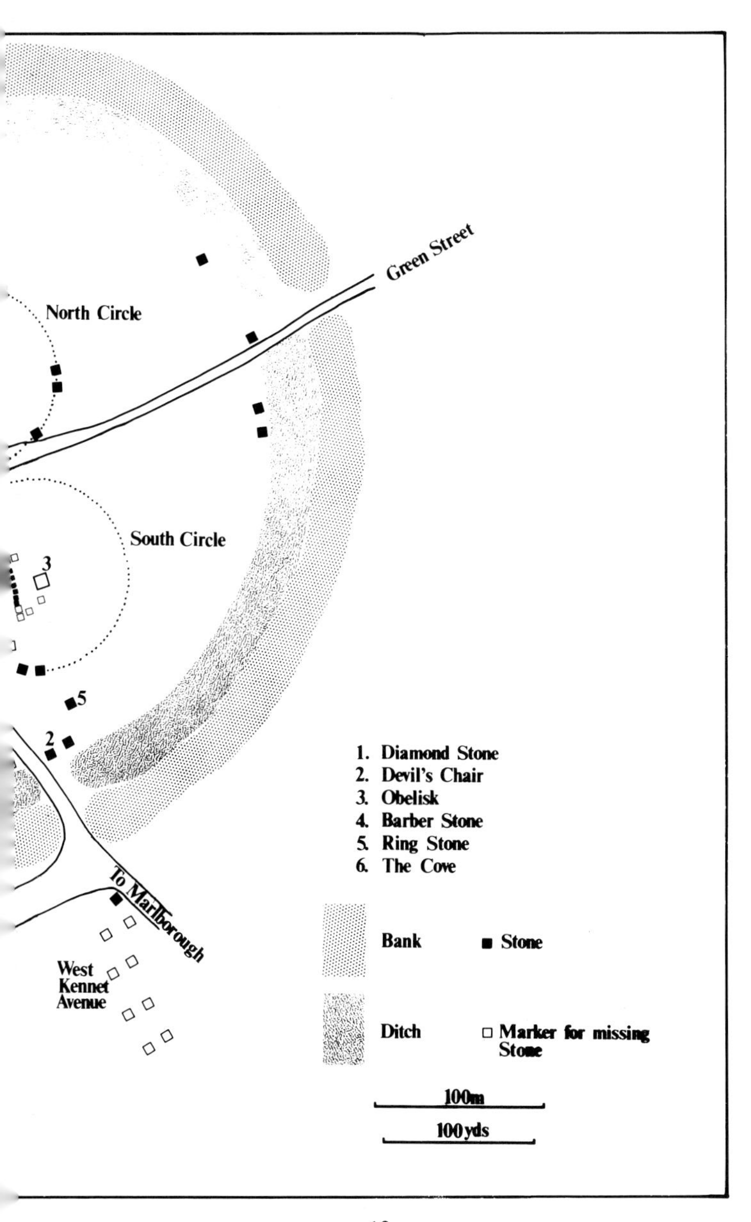
Green Street
North Circle
South Circle
3
5
2
To Marlborough
West
Kennet
Avenue
1. Diamond Stone
2. Devil's Chair
3. Obelisk
4. Barber Stone
5. Ring Stone
6. The Cove
Bank
Stone
Ditch
Marker for missing Stone
100m
100yds

Lion as far as the parish church, is a narrow cobbled pavement. This was laid down in the nineteenth century, when the High Street was no more than a chalk road, in order to provide the villagers with a dry path. On the other side of the road, an open drain (now covered in parts) runs the entire length of the High Street.

Opposite the central car park are the village **Post Office** and the **Craft Shop.** The steep pitch of the roof of the Craft Shop indicates that the building was once thatched. The tall chimneys were intended to keep sparks as far away from the thatch as possible.

Fire was always a danger in a thatched building. The **Manor Farm** opposite was once thatched. A fire at the beginning of the twentieth century destroyed the roof. An additional storey was added and a tiled roof replaced the thatch. One of the men engaged in the rebuilding was killed when the scaffolding collapsed and he was impaled on the iron railings in front of the house. On the other side of the road is the reconstructed sarsen stone found in the fabric of a now demolished cottage.

The small building with a corrugated roof standing next to the footpath was formerly thatched and was the wheelwright's workshop. Opposite are cottages of the nineteenth century, next to which is the manor gateway. A little further along on the other side of the road is the old village school.

3. The parish church of St James

The church is reached through the fine lychgate of 1899 and across the neat churchyard with its lichen-covered gravestones. The parish church of St James dates back to the period before the Norman conquest. The Anglo-Saxon settlers of Avebury built a small stone church. Fragments of this early place of Christian worship survive in the fabric of the present church, which is the product of various alterations and rebuildings over the centuries. The visitor enters the church through the south porch and Norman south doorway. The Anglo-Saxon church had a small rectangular nave with a short chancel. Five of the original windows of this early building still remain. Two unglazed round-headed windows of a lower range can be seen on each side of the nave near its west end. High above the arcade in the north wall of the nave, three of the four small circular windows of the upper range survive. It has been suggested that the concentric ring of small holes round each window was used to support a wattle framework during the construction of the inner splay of the window.

Aisles were added to the church in the twelfth century. However, the original openings from the nave were demolished

(Above) The village viewed from the south-west bank.

(Below) The parish church of St James.

Avebury Manor.

in 1812, when the present arcade was created. Remains of the Norman work appear in the wall at each end of the arcade. A lancet window of the thirteenth century pierces the west wall of the north aisle. A small number of medieval floor tiles can be seen amongst Victorian ones in the floor at the east end of each aisle. Here, a 'squint' in each aisle also allows a view of the main altar in the chancel. Although the rood screen is Victorian, the fine fifteenth-century rood loft above is a particularly rare survival of the Reformation, having been carefully concealed until it was discovered in 1810. The present chancel and chancel arch date from the thirteenth century, with Victorian reconstruction.

An early twelfth-century carved stone font occupies a central position at the base of the fifteenth-century tower. Nearby stands a large tenor bell weighing 1 ton. This huge bell was cast in 1719 in the Whitechapel Foundry by Richard Phelps, who was born in Avebury. Part of an old oak bell-frame with the carved date of 1636 was removed from the belfry and now sits at the base of the tower. A stone coffin of the thirteenth or fourteenth century lies in the corner.

On leaving the church it is a short walk to Avebury Manor. On the way, a small fragment of Anglo-Saxon cross shaft can be seen in the outside wall of the church, where the north side of the tower joins the aisle.

4. Avebury Manor

Avebury Manor is an attractive house built early in the reign of Queen Elizabeth I, with later additions of the early seventeenth century. The manor and its surrounding gardens are open to the public on a number of days during the year. After several changes in ownership in recent years, Avebury Manor is now under the welcomed protection of the National Trust.

The manor stands on or near the site of a small Benedictine cell of the twelfth century. Fragments of early carved stonework have been found in the manor gardens, and an area of the manor grounds is still known as Monks' Garden. Recent archaeological excavation is revealing evidence which will doubtless throw further light on the history of this period.

A stone flagged path leads across a tidy lawn to the front door in the gabled east front. This small unimposing doorway has now replaced the more impressive south porch as the main entrance to the house.

The manor has many interesting architectural features. The present entrance leads into the Little Parlour of 1560, which is the oldest part of the building. This room and the Elizabethan Great Parlour are both oak-panelled. The Queen Anne Dining Room was originally the Great Hall; Queen Anne herself is said to have dined in this room. On the upper floor, the finely carved fireplace and moulded plaster ceilings of the Elizabethan bedchamber are especially worthy of note.

The manor grounds are particularly attractive and have been maintained in a style in keeping with the house. There is a series of secluded walled gardens and some unusual and interesting topiary. Damask roses provide a spectacular display in their season, competing in colour with the peacocks which wander throughout the gardens. Near the south wall is a pets' graveyard, complete with headstones, where former manor pets are interred.

Avebury Manor has a number of ghosts. The Cavalier bedchamber is reputed to be haunted by a figure from the Civil War period, and a lady in white and a hooded figure, perhaps a monk, have also been seen on various occasions.

Whilst visitors are unlikely to see a ghost, they will find a house with a fascinating history, full of atmosphere.

5. Alexander Keiller Museum

The Alexander Keiller Museum is housed in the converted eighteenth-century stables which once belonged to the manor. An old stone mounting block stands close by. The museum was founded in 1938 by Alexander Keiller, who until his death in 1955 owned and lived in Avebury Manor. It houses the extensive collection of archaeological finds from Keiller's excavations in Avebury, Windhill and the West Kennet Avenue. Artefacts from subsequent excavations are also exhibited in the museum.

After Keiller's death the museum passed into the care of the National Trust. It is now under the guardianship of English Heritage and is open throughout the year. Members of the National Trust and of English Heritage are entitled to free admission.

The most striking feature on entering the museum is the rectangular glazed opening set into the floor at the centre of the building. Inside lies the small skeleton of a child who died before 3000 BC. The cause of death may have been hydrocephalus, or 'water on the brain'. The skeleton was found during excavations at Windmill Hill. He is affectionately called 'Charlie' by the custodians.

The museum was extensively redisplayed in 1991. Around the walls are glass-fronted exhibition cases which contain many of the most interesting finds from the Avebury excavations. There is a variety of pottery vessels and sherds, stone implements, the reconstructed skeletons of small domestic animals and neolithic bone digging tools. Accompanying texts, photographs, diagrams, drawings and models complete the displays.

Although the museum is compact, its collection of archaeological artefacts is rich and fascinating. A visit will provide the visitor with a detailed insight into the archaeological background of Avebury, the surrounding monuments and the work of Keiller and the later archaeologists. The custodians welcome questions and enquiries and are always pleased to help the visitor. Postcards, guidebooks, colour slides and souvenirs are on sale and membership of English Heritage can be taken out.

6. Avebury Dovecote

The Avebury Dovecote stands between the museum and the Great Barn. It is a small circular stone building with a conical roof, the apex of which has a round opening surmounted by another much smaller raised conical roof. This allowed easy access for the birds that lived within. The inside wall of the dovecote is lined with over five hundred nesting holes built into the thickness of the wall.

(Above) Alexander Keiller Museum.

(Below) Avebury Dovecote.

Several dozen beautiful white doves and the occasional wood pigeon still make use of this building as a safe home. The crumbs of food dropped by customers at the nearby restaurant help provide the birds with a regular diet.

During the midle ages the Lord of the Manor enjoyed the privilege of keeping a dovecote. Fresh meat was very scarce as most livestock had usually been slaughtered before winter. The doves provided a welcome alternative to salted meat.

The earliest documentary record of the Avebury Dovecote does not occur until 1595, when the building was the subject of a lawsuit over rival claims for its ownership. The dispute was finally settled in favour of Avebury Manor and the Dovecote remains manor property today.

7. The Great Barn Museum of Wiltshire Folk Life

The Great Barn is a fine thatched building of the late seventeenth century. It now houses the Museum of Wiltshire Folk Life. As well as providing the museum premises, the Great Barn is itself the oldest and largest of all the exhibits.

The barn was built around 1690. William Stukeley records that Lord Stawell, who at that time owned Avebury Manor, had levelled the earthen bank which surrounds that part of the circle where the barn now stands. It is suggested that the barn was constructed between the years 1683, when Lord Stawell was elevated to the peerage, and 1696, when he sold the manor. In Stukeley's time the barn was known as Parsonage Barn.

The Great Barn was a threshing barn, mainly used for the storage and threshing of corn. Wagons and horses were used to transport the harvested corn from the fields to the barn, where the threshing took place. The large pairs of opposite doors enabled the wagon to enter, unload and depart without having to turn round or back out. The through draught created between the doors separated the wheat from the chaff during winnowing, the lighter unwanted husks being blown away, leaving the grain behind.

The barn remained in use as a farm building until modern times. By the early 1960s the building had fallen into a state of disrepair and was in imminent danger of demolition. The intervention of several worthy people dedicated to the preservation of the building forestalled its destruction. The fate of the Great Barn was even debated in the House of Lords. Temporary repairs to the structure and thatch saved the building until a complete restoration could be contemplated. By the mid 1970s

(Above) The Great Barn.

(Below) The interior of the Great Barn and the displays of the Museum of Wiltshire Folk Life.

the barn had begun to outlive its usefulness to modern agriculture and was in grave need of extensive renovation. The Great Barn was then restored by the Wiltshire Folk Life Society to become the centre for its activities.

The Great Barn is 145 feet (44 m) long. Its aisled construction makes possible a roof span of over 36 feet (11 m) in width. The main structure of sturdy timbers of oak rests on a low wall of sarsen stone. The roof is thatched in wheat straw and covered with wire netting to protect it from damage by birds. The last thatching was completed in 1978 and, with minor attention, should be good for at least twenty years.

On entering the Great Barn, the visitor will immediately be aware of the rich rustic smell of the timber and thatch. There is also a noticeable drop in temperature. The barn is always much cooler inside than outside, which well illustrates the insulating properties of thatch. This helped to preserve the grain which was once stored in the barn.

The exhibitions in the Museum of Wiltshire Folk Life illustrate the social, domestic and agricultural life of the county of Wiltshire from the Victorian period until the early twentieth century. The aisled construction of the Great Barn divides the building into bays which provide a most natural setting for rural life material. Unlike most museums, none of the displays is in a glass case nor is the visitor kept at arm's length from the exhibits.

The reconstructions of the saddler's workshop, the blacksmith's forge and the wheelwright's workshop can be entered and the contents examined. The specialised craft tools are laid out on the workbenches with the part-finished and completed products of the craftsman's trade.

In another display there is a shepherd dressed in a typical Wiltshire smock and holding a crook. He stands next to a Wiltshire Horned ram. This rare breed of sheep was once plentiful on the Wiltshire downs and vital to the economy of the county.

An assortment of dairying equipment and utensils is used to help explain the process of making 'Wiltshire' cheese. The ropemaking machine was formerly used in Green Street in Avebury.

Additional displays and subjects include thatching, farm implements, traps and other rural topics. The museum also displays a life-sized photograph of the Avebury Giant. He was Fred Kempster, who was 8 feet 4 inches (2.54 m) tall, weighed over 27 stones (171 kg) and lived in the village during the early 1900s.

A regular programme of craft demonstrations takes place at weekends in the Great Barn throughout the season. Demonstrations range from the traditional, like coopering (barrel making), blacksmithing, spinning and sheep shearing, to modern crafts.

A well stocked museum shop sells a wide range of handmade craft goods, postcards, souvenirs and books. The award-winning local **Tourist Information Centre** adjoins the museum shop.

The south wing of the Great Barn was once a stable block, now converted into **Stones Restaurant**. The original structure was contemporary with the barn, but the building was substantially altered during the late nineteenth century. The former granary, which stands close by, now houses the **National Trust Shop**. It is a nineteenth-century building of brick and stone beneath a slate roof. A covered loading platform projects from the upper floor. The granary has been well restored and tastefully converted to the high standard expected from the National Trust.

The Avebury Monument is enjoyed by at least a quarter of a million people each year. Many of these people consider that the Avebury stone circle is still, today, of particularly mystical significance. Although most visitors come to see the prehistoric circle, they will also find a village with a rich and varied history, which has contributed to the character of this most fascinating of places.

Two of the remaining stones of The Cove.

Further reading

Burl, Aubrey. *Prehistoric Avebury*. Yale University Press, 1979.
Malone, Caroline. *Prehistoric Monuments of Avebury*. English Heritage, 1991.
Pitts, M. W. *Footprints through Avebury*. Stones Print, 1985.
Smith, Isobel. *Windmill Hill and Avebury*. Clarendon Press, 1965.
Victoria County History, Wiltshire. Oxford University Press, 1973.

Useful information

Avebury Tourist Information Centre. Telephone: 06723 425. Open: April to October, daily 10 to 6.

Alexander Keiller Museum. Telephone: 06723 250. Open Good Friday to 30th September, daily 10 to 6; 1st October to Maundy Thursday, daily 10 to 4. Closed Christmas Eve, Christmas Day, Boxing Day and New Year's Day.

The Great Barn Museum of Wiltshire Folk Life. Telephone: 06723 555. Open: April to October, daily 10 to 6; November to March, Saturdays 1 to 4.30, Sundays 11 to 4.30. At other times by appointment.

Avebury Manor. Telephone: 06723 251. Visitors are advised to check for opening times.

National Trust Shop. Telephone: 06723 384. Open: 1st April to 31st October, daily 11 to 5.45; 1st November to mid December, Saturdays and Sundays only 11 to 4.30.

Red Lion Inn. Telephone: 06723 266.

Stones Restaurant. Telephone: 06723 514.